REAL-LIFE ZOMBIES

EDGE BOOKS

MINI MIND CONTROLLERS

FUNGI, BACTERIA, AND OTHER TINY ZOMBIE MAKERS

BY JOAN AXELROD-CONTRADA

CONSULTANT:
BEN HANELT
RESEARCH ASSISTANT, PROFESSOR, AND LECTURER
DEPARTMENT OF BIOLOGY
UNIVERSITY OF NEW MEXICO
ALBUQUERQUE, NEW MEXICO

CAPSTONE PRESS
a capstone imprint

Edge Books are published by Capstone Press,
1710 Roe Crest Drive, North Mankato, Minnesota 56003
www.mycapstone.com

Cataloging-in-Publication Data
Cataloging-in-Publication Data is on file with the Library of Congress.
ISBN 978-1-5157-2478-0 (library binding)
ISBN 978-1-5157-2505-3 (eBook PDF)

Editorial Credits
Abby Colich, editor; Kyle Grenz, designer; Pam Mitsakos, media researcher;
Laura Manthe, production specialist

Photo Credits
Alamy: Natural Visions, 11; Alex Wild Photography/Alex Wild/alexanderwild.com,
20-21; Getty Images: DAVID M PHILLIPS, 24; Malcolm Storey, www.bioimages.
org.uk, 13; National Geographic Creative: ANAND VARMA, 8; Newscom: Kurt HP
Guek/NHPA/Photoshot, 23, Mark Moffett/Minden Pictures, cover; Insect Images:
Peggy Greb, USDA Agricultural Research Service, Bugwood.org, 19; Science Source:
Eye of Science, 26; Shutterstock: AuntSpray, 4, Contrail, 16, Florian Andronache,
25, Hein Nouwens, 27, J-R, 17, Kletr, 28, Pagina, 15, shunfa Teh, 1, Svetlana Rib, 5,
toeytoey, 29, Tree Vongvitavat, 14; Thinkstock: K-Kucharska_D-Kucharski, back
cover, 7

Design Elements: Shutterstock

Printed in the United States of America.
009680F16

TABLE OF CONTENTS

CASTING A ZOMBIE-MAKING SPELL

In the grasslands of Africa, a mosquito bites more people than usual. Why? It's no longer in control of its own actions. A tiny creature has taken over its mind.

It's as if the mosquito has turned into a zombie.

In books and movies, zombies are humans that rise from the dead. They walk the Earth with no control over their own behavior. Zombies aren't real. In nature, however, mind control happens often. These zombielike creatures are under the control of parasites.

Some of nature's zombie makers are tiny wormlike creatures. Others are life forms too small to see without a microscope. In their hosts these parasites find food and shelter. The host often dies in the process. Some parasites have more than one host. A few even trick one host into getting eaten by another.

Are these zombie-making parasites fascinating or terrifying? You decide.

parasite—an animal or plant that lives on or inside another animal or plant
host—a living plant or animal on which a parasite lives

THE ZOMBIE CATERPILLAR-EYED SNAIL

A small snail slips into the light of day. This snail is normally only active at night. Why the change? It's fallen under the spell of parasitic **flukes**.

The cycle begins when young flukes work their way inside of a snail. Inside the snail the flukes travel to the snail's eyestalk. The eyestalk swells and turns green. Then the flukes get to work making a zombie of the snail. Instead of hiding where it's dark and safe from **predators**, the mind-controlled snail comes out into the light. Now more birds can see it. To a passing bird, the green, swollen eyestalk looks like a tasty caterpillar.

fluke—a type of parasitic flatworm

predator—an animal that hunts other animals for food

a snail's eyestalk infected with flukes

A bird pecks away at the snail's eyestalk. Now inside the bird, the young flukes grow into adults.

FAST FACT The snail survives the attack. Its eyestalk grows back. The snail may even host another round of body-snatching flukes.

The flukes lay eggs inside their new host. The eggs come out with the bird's poop. Later these new, young flukes will find their next snail victim.

THE BERRY-BELLIED ZOMBIE ANT

In a rain forest, a worker ant feeds bird poop to young ants. Inside the poop are eggs of a tiny **roundworm**. Inside the ant, the eggs hatch. The tiny roundworms grow into adults. They take in food from the ant's outer skin. Soon the hard, black skin thins. It also changes color. Before long, the ant's belly looks like a ripe, red berry.

The adult roundworms lay eggs inside the ant's berry-looking belly.

roundworm—a type of small, parasitic worm
with a round body

Then the ant's behavior changes. Normally energetic, it becomes sluggish. The ant also spends more time than usual outside of the nest. It holds its berry-looking belly up in the air. A hungry bird flies by. Gulp! The bird plucks off the ant's stomach, thinking it's a juicy snack.

FAST FACT Scientists originally thought the red-bellied creatures were a new type of ant. Then they put them under a microscope. The scientists saw the tiny, wiggly worms!

The bird has eaten the ant's belly, roundworm eggs and all. Later the eggs come out with the bird's poop. The poop becomes food for more young ants.

Soon this body-snatching cycle will begin again.

ZOMBIE CRABS

On the seashore a young female **barnacle** sneaks into a crack in a green crab's shell. The barnacle grows tiny body parts that look like roots. The "roots" soak up food from the crab.

Inside its crab home, the barnacle grows into an adult.

Then the barnacle's mind-controlling powers turn on. It causes the crab to stop growing. The crab no longer produces young. All of the crab's energy goes to its parasite. The crab has become like a zombie.

barnacle—a small shellfish that attaches itself to the sides of ships

crab with a sac of barnacle eggs
attached to its abdomen

FAST FACT The barnacle even makes male crabs look and act like females. This assures that male crabs, too, will help nurture the barnacle's young.

The barnacle lays eggs in a sac outside of the crab's stomach. The eggs soon hatch. Young barnacles swim out into the water and find their own crab host.

THE YELLOW SHRINKING ZOMBIE ANT

In a tree in Western Europe, a worker ant feasts on bird poop. Inside the poop are the eggs of a **tapeworm**. Inside the ant, the eggs turn into **larvae**. The larvae quickly make a zombie of this ant. Normally brown, the ant turns yellow.

It shrinks in size. While other worker ants stay busy, the infected ant becomes lazy. It even starts to smell badly.

tapeworm—a parasitic flatworm, or simple worm with a soft flat body

larva—a stage of an insect's life between egg and adult

It's not just the infected ant that changes behavior. Other ants nearby act differently too. Scientists think the stink of their fellow ant confuses them. Instead of running from predators, the ants stick together. When the ants stick together, the infected ant is more likely to be eaten. And more likely the tapeworms inside of it will get to travel to their next host.

Soon a woodpecker licks up the ants. The tapeworms now live comfortably inside the woodpecker. Tapeworm eggs come out with the bird's poop. The egg-filled poop becomes dinner for another worker ant.

The zombie making begins again.

COLOR-CHANGING ZOMBIE SHRIMP

Imagine a parasite that tricks its host into going to a party to get eaten alive. Ghoulish? Perhaps, but the brine shrimp, also known as the sea monkey, has no choice but to go along.

The tapeworm living inside it is in control.

The cycle begins when shrimp eat bird poop. The poop is filled with tapeworm eggs. The eggs develop into larvae inside their hosts. Then the larvae brainwash the shrimp. Normally loners, the shrimp now gather together. Then the sneaky tapeworms turn the shrimp a pinkish red. One colorless shrimp might be overlooked. But a red swarm? It's impossible for a hungry flamingo to miss.

pink, tapeworm-infected brine shrimp

The flamingo gets a delicious shrimp dinner, tapeworms and all.

Inside the flamingo, the tapeworms grow into adults and **mate**. Later the flamingo poops out tapeworm eggs. A shrimp eats them, and the cycle starts again.

FAST FACT The flamingo gets its pink color from the pink shrimp it eats.

mate—to join together to produce young

ZOMBIE HORNETS

It's a hot summer day. A Japanese yellow hornet queen crawls into a rotting log. Normally, this hornet waits until fall to hide in the log for the winter. However, a sneaky roundworm has taken over her schedule—and her mind!

The tiny roundworm crawls into the hornet's body through the mouth or anus. Then it stops the host from mating. Now all the hornet's energy goes to its uninvited guest. The roundworm lays eggs inside the hornet.

The eggs hatch and grow into larvae.

When the larvae are ready to leave their host, the hornet poops them out. The young worms wait for a new queen hornet to come along. They sneak inside their new host. The zombie making starts again.

FAST FACT This roundworm spares its host's life. However, some roundworms aren't so nice. They eat their hosts' innards, and then burst out and kill them.

RED AND GLOWING LARVAE

A roundworm slyly slips inside an insect larva. This roundworm isn't picky. It can infect the larvae of beetles, moths, or butterflies. But this roundworm has a parasite of its own. Tiny **bacteria** live inside its body. Once the roundworm gets in the larva, the bacteria turn the larva red.

One type of moth larva even glows when infected!

FAST FACT

Gardeners and farmers use this roundworm as natural pest control. Farmers buy them by the millions. They spread them over their crop. The roundworms kill the pests. These farmers won't have to use harmful chemicals.

bacteria—single-celled, microscopic organisms that live everywhere in nature

Why the color change? Birds often feast on larvae. But they're less likely to pick up ones that are red or glowing. This gives the roundworm inside a better chance of survival. It would die if eaten by the bird.

Both the roundworm and bacteria feed off the larva. Then the roundworm kills its host. Inside the dead larva, the roundworm lays eggs. The eggs later hatch.

The corpse splits open. Tiny worms emerge.

They find new larvae hosts in the soil. Their color-changing life cycle begins again.

roundworms outside of a dead moth larva

ZOMBIE WASPS

A female wasp inserts her egg into a fly larva, or maggot. This wasp, in turn, has its own parasite—a **virus**. Inside the maggot a young wasp hatches. The female wasp usually finds a maggot that does not already have an egg inside. But the sneaky virus changes the wasp's behavior. The virus-infected female wasp finds a maggot already occupied with other wasp eggs.

virus—a germ that infects living things and causes diseases

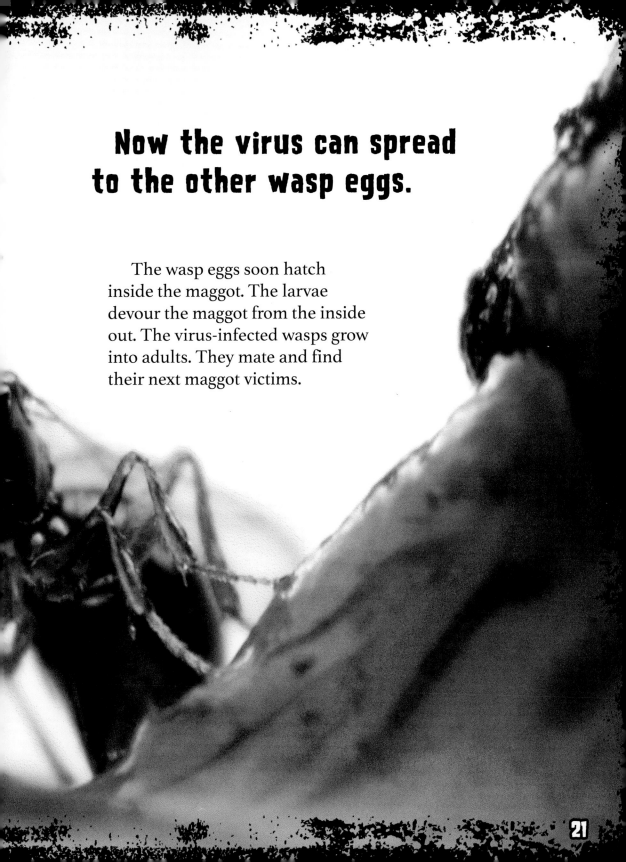

Now the virus can spread to the other wasp eggs.

The wasp eggs soon hatch inside the maggot. The larvae devour the maggot from the inside out. The virus-infected wasps grow into adults. They mate and find their next maggot victims.

HEAD-EXPLODING ZOMBIE ANT

In a rain forest, a carpenter ant stumbles around in a daze. A **fungus** has taken over its brain. The fungi release chemicals that control the ant's behavior. Carpenter ants usually hang out near their nests. But a fungi-controlled ant leaves. It travels to higher, warmer, more humid areas.

Here the fungi can more easily spread.

The fungi also force the ant to bite onto a leaf. It can't let go. Now the fungi can do their dirty work. The fungi release deadly chemicals that kill the ant. Then the fungi burst out of the ant's head. The fluffy fungi jut into the sky. They spread farther than if they were released closer to the ground.

fungus—a type of living thing that has no leaves, flowers, or roots

Ants have a defense against the fungi. They groom themselves by picking off the fungi. Unfortunately, the ants can't always get rid of it all. Some ants have learned to move a fungus-infected ant far away. This helps keep the other ants safe.

Fungus to the Rescue!

Some zombie-makers get a dose of their own medicine. The fungi that make zombies of the carpenter ant sometimes have their own parasite—another fungus! The second fungus grows on top of its fellow fungi and eats away. The attack prevents the original fungus from spreading. As a result, ants are protected.

Now the fungi have a better chance of infecting more ants.

23

ZOMBIE CATERPILLAR GOO

A gypsy moth caterpillar climbs a tree in broad daylight. Normally, the caterpillar hides during the day. But earlier it ate leaves covered with the baculovirus. With this virus now inside its body, the caterpillar has no control over its own behavior. Scientists think the virus takes over the caterpillar's eating habits. No longer in charge of when it eats, the caterpillar climbs a tree to feed on leaves. Soon it dies.

baculovirus

Its body turns to dripping goo.

Gypsy moths devour tree leaves. They damage roughly 1 million acres of forest every year. Some trees are sprayed with baculovirus. The baculovirus helps protect trees from the damage caused by gypsy moth caterpillars.

gypsy moth caterpillar

The virus oozes down the leaves. Other gypsy moth caterpillars eat the gooey leaves. The virus lives on in its new victims.

TSETSE FLY VICTIMS

Tsetse is a large fly found in Africa. The fly bites people and other animals, sucking up their blood. But the tsetse doesn't travel alone. Inside its body is a tiny protozoan.

the protozoan that causes African sleeping sickness

The protozoan causes a disease that's deadly to humans.

It begins when a tsetse bites a victim who already hosts the protozoan. The protozoan matures inside the fly. When the tsetse feeds again, the protozoan moves from the fly into to its next victim.

protozoan—a tiny, microscopic animal

The protozoan changes the behavior of its hosts. It causes sleepiness during the day. That is when a tsetse fly bites most often. Now the protozoan can find its way into more victims.

Mother's Milk for Young Flies

In some ways, tsetse flies resemble humans. Like human mothers, they give birth to one offspring at a time. They nurse their young. Tsetse milk even contains proteins similar to those in human milk. Researchers hope to someday slow the spread of African sleeping sickness by reducing the tsetse's ability to produce milk.

What happens when the protozoan enters a human? It causes African sleeping sickness. The disease causes sleeplessness at night. Victims are overcome by sleepiness during the day. They become irritable, confused, and sometimes violent. If left untreated, nearly all people die from the disease.

ZOMBIE MOSQUITOES

In the heat of the African sun, a female mosquito is hungry for human blood.

She needs the blood for her eggs. But she's not traveling alone. A crafty protozoan lives inside her. The protozoan flicks a switch in its host's body. The switch tells the female mosquito to hold off on biting humans.

FAST FACT Malaria infects more than 200 million people every year. Hundreds of thousands of them will die. The number of infections and deaths have declined in recent years. This is due to efforts to prevent the disease and treat it earlier with better medicines.

The protozoan isn't ready for its next host. It needs more time to grow. The mosquito gets the message. She waits before going after her next bloody meal. When it's ready, the protozoan sends a new command. Bite now! Then the parasite causes the mosquito to bite more than normal. The protozoan can now spread to more people.

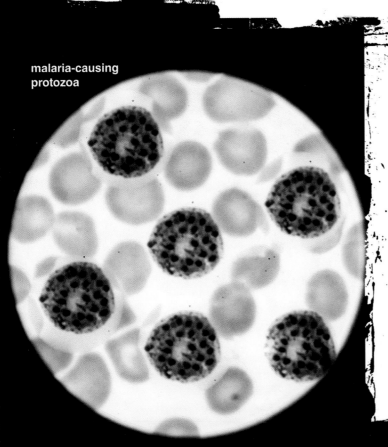

malaria-causing protozoa

Once inside a human, the protozoan causes the disease malaria. The victim has bouts of fever, chills, and sweating. Sometimes a protozoan lies dormant for months or even years. Then, like a creature rising from the dead, the protozoan causes a relapse of the disease.

To see real-life zombies, just look outside. Mind control is everywhere!

GLOSSARY

bacteria (bak-TEER-ee-uh)—single-celled, microscopic organisms that live everywhere in nature

barnacle (BAR-ni-kuhl)—a small shellfish that attaches itself to the sides of ships

fluke (FLUKE)—a type of parasitic flatworm

fungus (FUHN-guhs)—a type of living thing that has no leaves, flowers, or roots

host (HOHST)—a living plant or animal on which a parasite lives

larva (LAR-vuh)—a stage of an insect's life between egg and adult

mate (MATE)—to join together to produce young

parasite (PAIR-uh-site)—an animal or plant that lives on or inside another animal or plant

predator (PRED-uh-tur)—an animal that hunts other animals for food

protozoan (prote-uh-ZOE-uhn)—a tiny, microscopic animal

roundworm (ROWND-wurm)—a type of small, parasitic worm with a round body

tapeworm (TAPE-wurm)—a parasitic flatworm, or simple worm with a soft flat body

virus (VYE-ruhss)—a germ that infects living things and causes diseases

READ MORE

Goldsworthy, Steve. *Zombies: The Truth Behind History's Terrifying Flesh-Eaters.* Monster Handbooks. North Mankato, Minn.: Capstone Press, 2016.

Hirschmann, Kris. *Real Life Zombies.* New York: Scholastic Inc., 2013.

Johnson, Rebecca L. *Zombie Makers: True Stories of Nature's Undead.* Minneapolis, Minn.: Millbrook Press, 2013.

Larson, Kirsten W. *Zombies in Nature.* Freaky Nature. Mankato, Minn.: Amicus Ink, 2015.

INTERNET SITES

FactHound offers a safe, fun way to find Internet sites related to this book. All of the sites on FactHound have been researched by our staff.

Here's all you do:

Visit *www.facthound.com*

Type in this code: 9781515724780

Super-cool stuff!

Check out projects, games and lots more at
www.capstonekids.com

INDEX